ISAAC ASIMOV'S NEW LIBRARY OF THE UNIVERSE

PLANET OF EXTREMES: JUPITER

BY ISAAC ASIMOV
WITH REVISIONS AND UPDATING BY GREG WALZ-CHOJNACKI

Gareth Stevens Publishing
MILWAUKEE

For a free color catalog describing Gareth Stevens' list of high-quality books, call 1-800-542-2595 (USA) or 1-800-461-9120 (Canada). Gareth Stevens' Fax: (414) 225-0377.

Library of Congress Cataloging-in-Publication Data

Asimov, Isaac.
  Planet of extremes: Jupiter / by Isaac Asimov ; with revisions and updating by Greg Walz-Chojnacki.
      p. cm. — (Isaac Asimov's New library of the universe)
  Rev. ed. of: Jupiter: the spotted giant. 1989.
  Includes index.
  ISBN 0-8368-1222-0
  1. Jupiter (Planet)—Juvenile literature. [1. Jupiter (Planet).]
I. Walz-Chojnacki, Greg, 1954-. II. Asimov, Isaac. Jupiter: the spotted giant. III. Title. IV. Series: Asimov, Isaac. New library of the universe.
QB661.A845   1995
523.4'5—dc20   95-7880

This edition first published in 1995 by
Gareth Stevens Publishing
1555 North RiverCenter Drive, Suite 201
Milwaukee, Wisconsin 53212, USA

Revised and updated edition © 1995 by Gareth Stevens, Inc.
Original edition published in 1989 by Gareth Stevens, Inc. under the title
Jupiter: The Spotted Giant. Text © 1995 by Nightfall, Inc.
End matter and revisions © 1995 by Gareth Stevens, Inc.

Series editor: Barbara J. Behm
Design adaptation: Helene Feider
Production director: Teresa Mahsem
Editorial assistant: Diane Laska
Picture research: Matthew Groshek and Diane Laska

Printed in the United States of America

1 2 3 4 5 6 7 8 9 99 98 97 96 95

To bring this classic of young people's information up to date, the editors at Gareth Stevens Publishing have selected two noted science authors, Greg Walz-Chojnacki and Francis Reddy. Walz-Chojnacki and Reddy coauthored the recent book *Celestial Delights: The Best Astronomical Events Through 2001.*

Walz-Chojnacki is also the author of the book *Comet: The Story Behind Halley's Comet* and various articles about the space program. He was an editor of *Odyssey*, an astronomy and space technology magazine for young people, for eleven years.

Reddy is the author of nine books, including *Halley's Comet, Children's Atlas of the Universe, Children's Atlas of Earth Through Time*, and *Children's Atlas of Native Americans*, plus numerous articles. He was an editor of *Astronomy* magazine for several years.

CONTENTS

We live in an enormously large place – the Universe. It's just in the last fifty-five years or so that we've found out how large it probably is. It's only natural that we would want to understand the place in which we live, so scientists have developed instruments – such as radio telescopes, satellites, probes, and many more – that have told us far more about the Universe than could possibly be imagined.

We have seen planets up close. We have learned about quasars and pulsars, black holes, and supernovas. We have gathered amazing data about how the Universe may have come into being and how it may end. Nothing could be more astonishing.

The largest planet in our Solar System is Jupiter, grandly named for the king of gods in ancient Roman myths. Jupiter is an enormous world that dwarfs our own Earth. In fact, everything about the planet is extreme – its atmosphere, its storms, its temperatures, and its sixteen natural satellites, or moons. And recent comet collisions on Jupiter have made this planet even more thrilling!

Isaac Asimov

The Bright Planet Jupiter

Jupiter is the fourth brightest object in the sky. Only the Sun, Earth's Moon, and Venus are brighter.

In 1610, an Italian scientist, Galileo Galilei, spotted Jupiter through a small telescope. Near the planet, he saw four dimmer objects. Night after night, the objects moved back and forth from one side of Jupiter to the other.

These objects turned out to be satellites, or moons, of Jupiter. They circle Jupiter the way our Moon circles Earth.

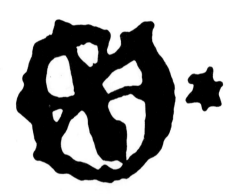

Above: Galileo's sketches of Jupiter and its moons.

Right: Galileo was an Italian astronomer who discovered Jupiter.

Opposite: Galileo saw Jupiter's moons through his homemade telescopes. Today, these moons can be seen with a good pair of binoculars *(inset).*

TVBVM·OPTICVM·VIDES·GALILAEI·INVENTVM·ET·OPVS,QVO·SOLIS·MACVLAS,
ET·EXTIMOS·LVNAE·MONTES·ET·IOVIS·SATELLITES,ET·NOVAM·QVASI
RERVM·VNIVERSITATE·PRIMVS·DISPEXIT·A.MDCIX.

Illuminating Jupiter

Jupiter orbits the Sun about once every twelve years. It stays in the zodiac. The zodiac is an imaginary belt in the sky containing the paths of the Sun, our Moon, and most of the planets. The zodiac is divided into twelve equal parts. Each part is named for a constellation.

When Jupiter is viewed through a small telescope, it looks like a little disk of light. Nearby are Jupiter's four largest satellites, some on one side of the planet, some on the other. From night to night, the positions of the satellites change as they move around Jupiter.

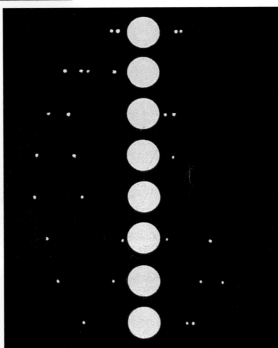

Left, top: To spot Jupiter, a clear night and a pair of good binoculars or a telescope are needed.

Left, bottom: Jupiter and its four largest moons as viewed through a small telescope.

Inset: Jupiter's four largest moons play hide-and-seek as they circle their parent planet over the course of eight nights, June 1 *(top)* through June 8 *(bottom)*.

7

A Closer Look

With a diameter of 88,735 miles (142,800 kilometers), Jupiter is the largest planet in our Solar System. Jupiter is more than 11 times wider than Earth, and it has the volume of 1,000 Earths. Even though Jupiter is so large, it spins much faster than Earth spins. Earth makes one full turn on its axis in twenty-four hours. Jupiter makes a full turn in just under ten hours.

Space probes, such as *Pioneers 10* and *11* and *Voyagers 1* and *2*, have flown past Jupiter. These probes have taken close-up photographs of Jupiter's surface. They have shown that the planet is a huge ball of the two simplest gases – mostly hydrogen plus some helium. The upper atmosphere also contains vapors of substances such as water, methane, and ammonia.

Opposite: A rocky core, about the size of Earth, may lie at Jupiter's center. Above the core is a vast layer of liquid hydrogen, making up most of Jupiter's mass. The upper atmosphere contains water, methane, and ammonia vapors.

Below: Jupiter outweighs all the other planets in the Solar System put together.

The heavyweight champ of the Solar System

Jupiter is so large that it is over three times as massive as Saturn, the next largest planet. Imagine you have a huge scale. Now put Jupiter in one of the pans of the scale. In the other pan, imagine you pile up all the other planets, satellites, asteroids, and comets. All of them put together would not balance the scale. Jupiter is more than twice as massive as all the other planetary material in the Solar System put together!

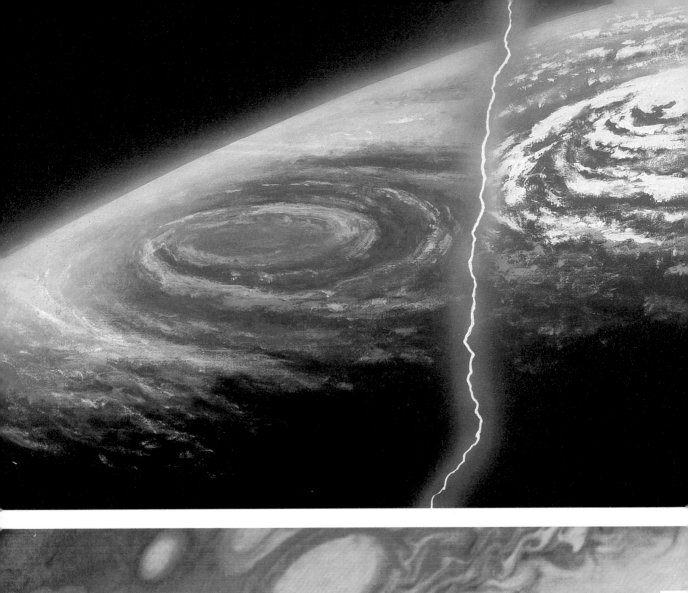

The Great Red Spot

Jupiter's surface is covered in dark "belts" with lighter "zones" between them. These areas are created by atmospheric movements. Vast winds move downward in the belts and upward in the zones.

Along the belts and zones are light and dark oval spots that are actually enormous whirling storm winds. The largest of these is called the Great Red Spot. It looks like a gigantic tornado or hurricane that never stops. Astronomers have watched it whirling for over three hundred years.

Top: Jupiter's Great Red Spot *(left)* and a storm on Earth *(right)* are similar in appearance, but not size.

Bottom: The Great Red Spot is so huge it could engulf three Earths!

! The Great Red Spot – nothing on Earth can compare!

Jupiter's Great Red Spot is enormous. Its dimensions are about 25,000 miles (40,000 km) from east to west and 8,000 miles (13,000 km) from north to south. Three Earth-size planets could fit side by side into the huge storm without touching the edges. The total area of the Great Red Spot is 175,000,000 square miles (453,250,000 sq. km).

11

Ring around the Planet

Material in space near the giant planets condenses, or collects, to form natural satellites, or moons. If this material is too close to a planet, however, the planet's gravity keeps the material from condensing. The material then forms a ring of small pieces around the planet.

The planet Saturn has very large, bright rings around it. Astronomers have known about Saturn's rings since the 1600s, when Galileo first saw them through his telescope.

But Jupiter had a surprise for astronomers – a surprise that went undetected until 1979. That's when *Voyager 1* discovered a thin ring about 30,000 miles (48,000 km) above Jupiter's cloudy edge. Jupiter's ring is too dim to be seen from Earth.

In addition, Jupiter has at least one small moon called a "shepherd" satellite. This moon's gravity keeps Jupiter's ring from spreading outward and disappearing.

❓ *The Great Red Spot – a storm with a mind of its own?*

Many mysteries surround the Great Red Spot. For one thing, scientists are not certain why it has lasted for centuries. Other storms come and go, but the Great Red Spot seems to be permanent. Scientists also wonder about the Great Red Spot's movements. It can move ahead or fall behind the rest of the clouds. It moves east and west, but not north and south.

Left: The view from Jupiter's ring. Sunlight scattered by the ring's tiny particles creates the appearance of a rainbow in space.

Left: *Voyager's* cameras photographed part of Jupiter's ring in 1979.

Top: Jupiter's ring is too faint to be seen from Earth. An artist added a ring to this picture of Jupiter to show the ring's size and location.

13

The Moons of Jupiter

Jupiter has sixteen known natural satellites, or moons. Of these, the four largest are called the Galilean satellites in honor of Galileo. But the satellites were named by a German astronomer, Simon Marius, who actually spotted them a few days before Galileo did. The nearest of the Galilean moons to Jupiter is Io. Beyond Io are Europa, Ganymede, and Callisto. Each of these moons is about the size of Earth's Moon, or larger.

Closer to Jupiter than its four large satellites is a small satellite called Amalthea, which is about 125 miles (201 km) across. Near it are three even smaller moons discovered by probes.

Far outside the orbits of the Galilean satellites are at least eight smaller moons. They range in size from 12 to 105 miles (19 to 169 km) across. These moons are probably captured asteroids.

Opposite: Jupiter and the Galilean satellites are shown not according to size but in their correct positions. *(Clockwise from upper left:)* Callisto, Ganymede, Io, Europa, and Jupiter.

Inset and below: Who's who in the Jupiter system? The orbits of Jupiter's moons, big and small, are shown.

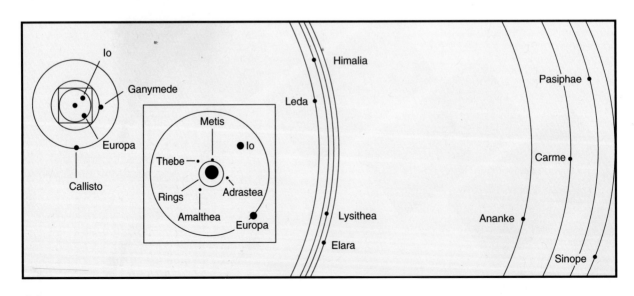

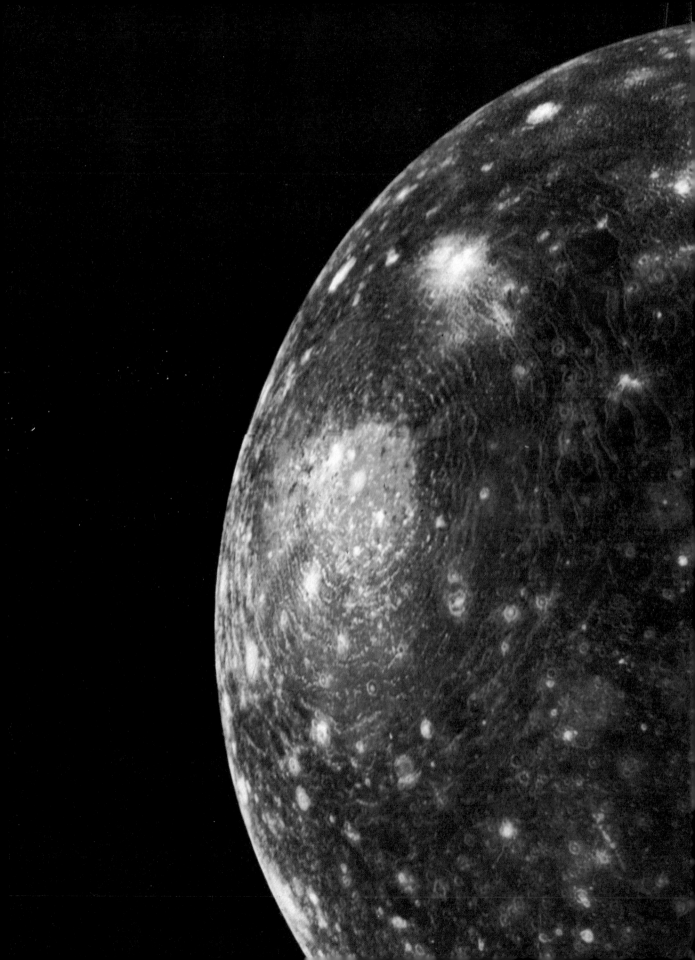

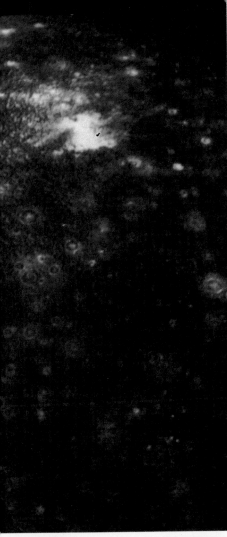

Icy and Cratered Callisto

Callisto, the farthest of the Galilean satellites from Jupiter, is 1,170,000 miles (1,883,000 km) from the planet. That's almost five times as far as our Moon is from Earth. Callisto orbits Jupiter in about 16 2/3 days.

Probes have shown that Callisto is a big ball of ice with some rock that may have a rocky core. Callisto is covered with craters. This is because billions of years ago, when it was first created, Callisto was bombarded by the final chunks of matter that formed it.

The craters are not very deep on Callisto because the icy surface slowly flowed and settled. But the flow wasn't enough to eliminate the craters entirely.

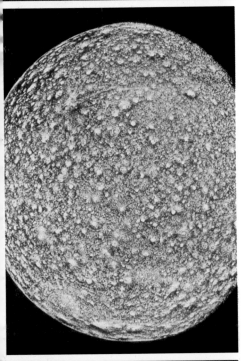

Left: The icy, fractured surface of Callisto, photographed by *Voyager 1* in 1979. Notice the bright ringed region near the moon's left edge – the remains of a violent impact that partially melted Callisto's frozen surface. This region is about 185 miles (300 km) across.

Inset: Callisto's craters revealed by *Voyager* probes.

Above: Callisto is a huge ball of ice. The objects that bombarded Callisto to form craters made so much heat that Callisto's surface partially melted and then refroze.

17

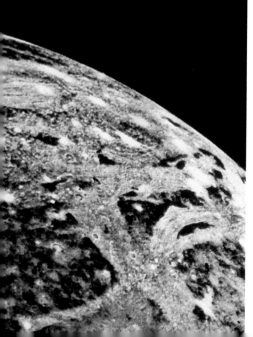
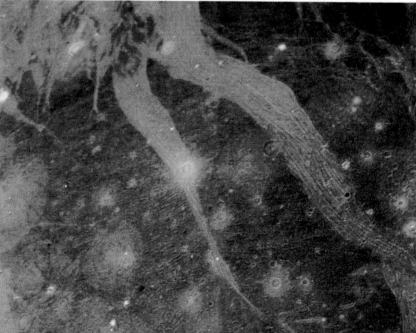

The Solar System's Largest Moon – Ganymede

Ganymede, the largest moon in the Solar System, is nearly 3,279 miles (5,276 km) across. It is larger than the planet Mercury. Like Callisto, Ganymede is mostly ice with some rock.

It takes Ganymede just over a week to orbit its planet. Ganymede is 665,000 miles (1,070,000 km) from Jupiter. This moon is not as thickly covered with craters as Callisto. That may be because Ganymede's crust seems to have cracked and shifted in many places over a long period of time. Water from inside Ganymede may have welled up, flooded many craters, and then froze smoothly over the surface.

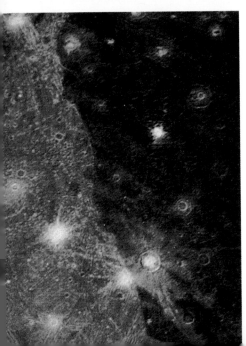

Top: A view of Jupiter from Ganymede, the largest satellite in our Solar System.

Opposite, bottom, left: The terrain of Ganymede is grooved. The grooves are caused by slow expansion and movement of the moon's crust.

Left: Craters old and new pepper Ganymede. The bright patches are fresh craters. The fainter circular markings may be ancient craters smoothed over by glacierlike flows on Ganymede's icy surface.

Fire and Ice: Two Volcanic Worlds

Io and Europa are the Galilean moons closest to Jupiter. Both are volcanic. Io erupts with molten rock; Europa with water.

Io is a rocky world a bit bigger than Earth's Moon. It orbits Jupiter every 1 3/4 days at a distance of about 262,000 miles (421,600 km) from the planet. As Io orbits Jupiter, the huge planet's gravity stretches Io slightly. This heats the moon's inner rock. The rock melts and eventually explodes in eruptions that shoot gas and sulfur high into the sky. Io gets its yellow coloring from the yellow sulfur that has erupted from within.

Europa, the smallest of the Galilean moons, is about 1,942 miles (3,125 km) across. About 417,000 miles (671,000 km) from Jupiter, it completes one orbit every 3.5 days. Its surface is covered with ice. Underneath the ice may be a sea of water. The water oozes out occasionally to cover any craters formed by meteorites. Some scientists have wondered if the water could contain life as we know it, but there is no evidence for this.

Opposite: Europa's smooth, icy surface is scarred by the impact of countless meteorites. This photo was taken by *Voyager 2.*

Below, left: An artist's concept of an ice-water volcano on Europa. Could a gigantic ocean lie beneath Europa's icy surface?

Below, right: Just as in space, parts of Earth are covered with ice. An ice field lies off Antarctica's coast.

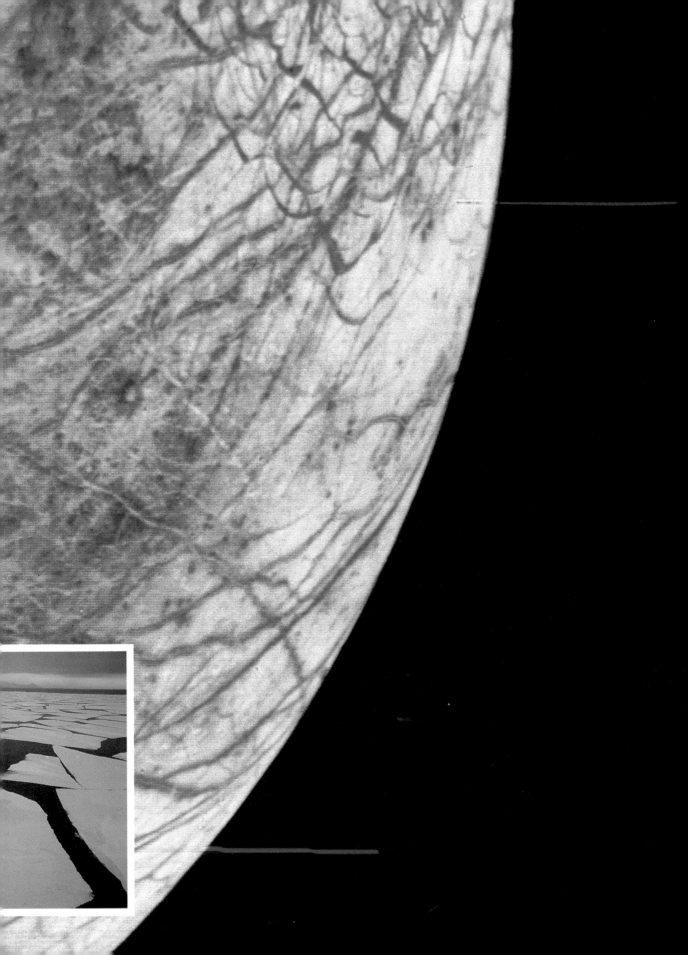

Probing the Planet Jupiter

Probes have provided astronomers with a great deal of information about Jupiter. Because of probes, we now know that Jupiter is surrounded by a magnetic field much larger and stronger than Earth's. The field is so strong and collects so many charged particles that it will be necessary for spaceships with humans aboard to stay far away from Jupiter.

The probes have also revealed that although temperatures surrounding Jupiter's cloud layer are very low, temperatures rise rapidly beneath the clouds. Thousands of miles below the cloud layer, Jupiter is hotter than the surface of the Sun!

Opposite: An artist's concept of a spectacular display in Jupiter's nighttime sky. The fierce lightning and streamers of light surpass in size and brilliance anything likely to be seen in Earth's atmosphere.

Inset: A computer image of Jupiter's intense magnetic field *(in blue).* Also shown is a trail of sulfur *(in yellow)* left by Io, a volcanic moon of Jupiter.

! *Jupiter – brought to you in living color*

Jupiter is a very colorful planet. The belts are orange, yellow, and brown. There are white spots, and, of course, the Great Red Spot, which isn't always red. Sometimes, the Great Red Spot's color pales until it can hardly be seen. Scientists are not certain what causes all the colors. They will obtain answers when instruments are placed into Jupiter's atmosphere.

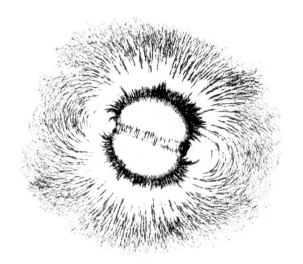

Above: A magnetic field can be created by placing a magnet under a sheet of paper covered with iron filings.

22

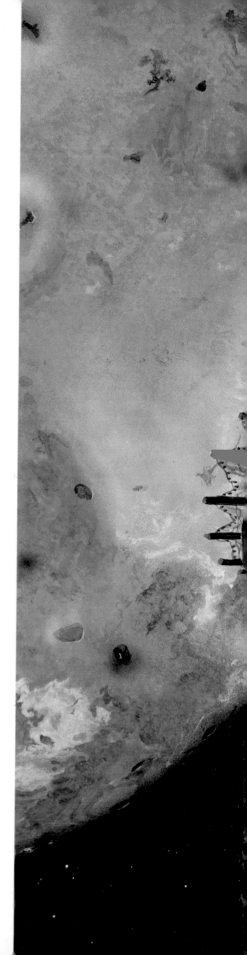

A Crippled Probe to Jupiter

Since 1980, all the outer planets (except Pluto) have been visited by spacecraft. As the spacecraft flew quickly past the planets, photographs were taken that provided valuable information to scientists. While these missions were very successful, the next step is to put spacecraft in orbit around these planets for weeks or months, so even more can be learned.

The first such journey will be to Jupiter. The *Galileo* mission already in space will descend toward Jupiter in December of 1995. For the following twenty-two months, *Galileo* will send data about Jupiter back to Earth. The probe will be sent directly into the planet's atmosphere, giving scientists a new look beneath the cloud tops.

Unfortunately, this brave new probe suffered a serious malfunction shortly after launch. The large umbrella-shaped antenna that is necessary for sending photos back to Earth failed to open completely. This means that the probe's data will be sent with a much smaller antenna, and the expected flood of new information will be more like a trickle.

With luck, the antenna will pop open when the speeding probe slows down to go into orbit.

Right: Galileo will take a looping excursion of Jupiter and its moons. This drawing shows the probe, with its malfunctioning antenna, on a visit to Io.

Smash Hits:
A Comet Collides with Jupiter

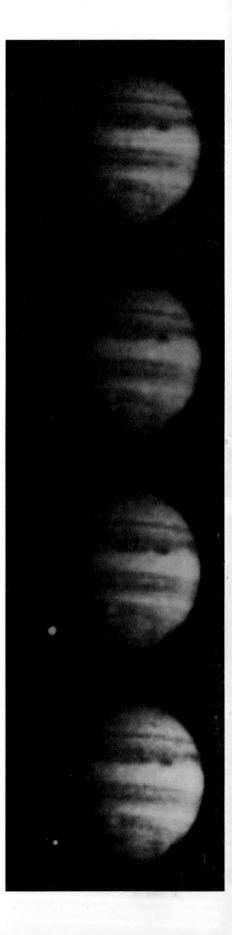

In July, 1994, twenty-one pieces of a comet collided with Jupiter. Tremendous explosions "excavated" the cloud tops of Jupiter, giving astronomers another way to see what lies below.

The comet pieces struck on the side of Jupiter not visible from Earth. But as the planet turned, the areas the comet hit came into view. With telescopes, such as the Hubble Space Telescope, astronomers could look at the dark "bruises" on Jupiter the collisions created. Even the *Galileo* spacecraft got into the act. It was on the far side of the planet, and actually "saw" one of the explosions.

Right: The *Galileo* spacecraft took these four snapshots when comet pieces struck Jupiter on July 22, 1994. The photos capture the moment when the final large fragment, called *W*, impacted.

Opposite, top: An artist's view of comet fragments hitting Jupiter's cloud tops. These were the biggest explosions ever seen by humans.

Opposite, bottom, left: One of Jupiter's "black eyes" made by a fragment of a comet. Each explosion had more energy than all the world's nuclear weapons combined!

Opposite, bottom, right: In this infrared or "heat" image, the bright spots reveal where comet fragments struck Jupiter.

?! *Jupiter's center – an inner Sun?*

Some scientists think Jupiter may be made of hydrogen and helium all the way through the planet. But many others do not think these gases are present all the way to the center. They think there is a ball of rock and metal at the very center the size of Earth, but right now there's no way of knowing for certain. Then, too, the center may be squeezed so hard that heat is produced there. Jupiter produces more heat than it receives from the Sun.

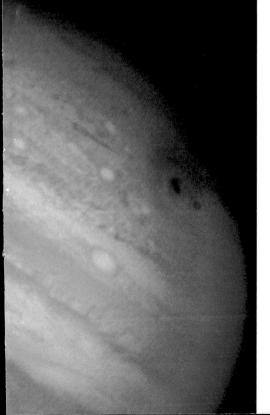
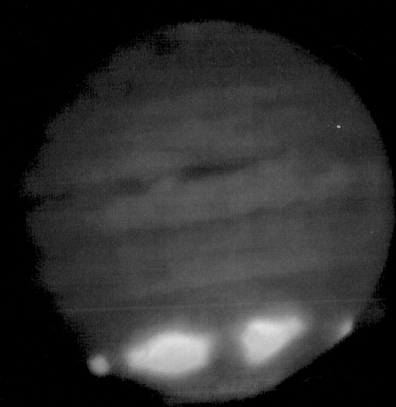

The Moons of Jupiter

Name	Metis	Adrastea	Amalthea	Thebe	Io	Europa
Diameter	25 miles* (40 km)*	15 miles (24 km)	125 miles** (201 km)**	62 miles (100 km)	2,255 miles (3,630 km)	1,942 miles (3,125 km)
Distance from Jupiter's Center	79,500 miles (128,000 km)	80,000 miles (128,700 km)	112,700 miles (181,300 km)	137,900 miles (221,900 km)	262,000 miles (421,600 km)	416,960 miles (671,000 km)
Name	Ganymede	Callisto	Leda	Himalia	Lysithea	Elara
Diameter	3,279 miles (5,276 km)	2,995 miles (4,820 km)	12 miles (20 km)	105 miles (170 km)	19 miles (30 km)	47 miles (76 km)
Distance from Jupiter's Center	665,000 miles (1,070,000 km)	1,170,000 miles (1,883,000 km)	6,904,000 miles (11,110,000 km)	7,127,500 miles (11,470,000 km)	7,277,000 miles (11,710,000 km)	7,295,000 miles (11,740,000 km)
Name	Ananke	Carme	Pasiphae	Sinope		
Diameter	19 miles (30 km)	25 miles (40 km)	31 miles (50 km)	25 miles (40 km)		
Distance from Jupiter's Center	12,863,000 miles (20,700,000 km)	13,888,000 miles (22,350,000 km)	14,479,000 miles (23,300,000 km)	14,727,000 miles (23,700,000 km)	* Estimated diameter ** Diameter at widest point	

Fact File: Jupiter, the Largest Planet

Our Solar System's largest known planet, Jupiter, is the fifth closest to the Sun. Like the Sun, Jupiter is mostly hydrogen and helium. Scientists believe the temperature at its core might be as much as 55,000°F (30,500°C). When it was formed over 4.5 billion years ago, Jupiter might have given off 10 million times as much energy as it does now. Jupiter was never massive enough to begin the process stars use to burn their hydrogen. But billions of years ago, it might have glowed like a miniature star!

Above: The Sun and its Solar System family, *left to right:* Mercury, Venus, Earth, Mars, Jupiter, Saturn, Uranus, Neptune, and Pluto.

Left: A close-up of Jupiter and its seven largest moons *(left to right),* Himalia, Callisto, Ganymede, Europa, Io, Thebe, and Amalthea.

Jupiter: How It Measures Up to Earth

Planet	Diameter	Rotation Period	Period of Orbit around Sun (length of year)	Moons	Surface Gravity
Jupiter	88,735 miles (142,800 km)	9 hours, 50.4 minutes	11.86 years	at least 16	2.53*
Earth	7,927 miles (12,756 km)	23 hours, 56 minutes	365.25 days (one year)	1	1.00*

Planet	Distance from Sun (nearest-farthest)	Least Time It Takes for Light to Travel to Earth	
Jupiter	460.4-506.9 million miles (740.9-815.7 million km)	32.75 minutes	
Earth	91-94 million miles (147-152 million km)	—	* Multiply your weight by this number to find out how much you would weigh on this planet.

More Books about Jupiter

Discovering Comets and Meteors. Asimov (Gareth Stevens)
Exploring Outer Space: Rockets, Probes, and Satellites. Asimov (Gareth Stevens)
The Giant Planets. Nourse (Franklin Watts)
Jupiter. Simon (Morrow Junior Books)
Our Planetary System. Asimov (Gareth Stevens)
Our Wonderful Solar System. Adams (Troll)
The Planets. Couper (Franklin Watts)

Videos

Astronomy 101: A Beginner's Guide to the Night Sky. (Mazon)
Comets and Meteors. (Gareth Stevens)
Jupiter: The Spotted Giant. (Gareth Stevens)

Places to Visit

You can explore Jupiter and other parts of the Universe without leaving Earth. Here are some museums and centers where you can find a variety of space exhibits.

NASA Lewis Research Center
Educational Services Office
21000 Brookpark Road
Cleveland, OH 44135

Henry Crown Science Center
Museum of Science and Industry
57th Street and Lake Shore Drive
Chicago, IL 60637

Edmonton Space and Science Centre
11211 - 142nd Street
Edmonton, Alberta K5M 4A1

Australian Museum
6-8 College Street
Sydney, NSW 2000 Australia

National Air and Space Museum
Smithsonian Institution
Seventh and Independence Avenue SW
Washington, D.C. 20560

The Space and Rocket Center
and Space Camp
One Tranquility Base
Huntsville, AL 35807

Places to Write

Here are some places you can write for more information about Jupiter. Be sure to state what kind of information you would like. Include your full name and address for a reply.

The Planetary Society
65 North Catalina
Pasadena, CA 91106

Sydney Observatory
P. O. Box K346
Haymarket 2000 Australia

NASA Jet Propulsion Laboratory
Public Affairs 180-201
4800 Oak Grove Drive
Pasadena, CA 91109

Canadian Space Agency
Communications Department
6767 Route de L'Aeroport
Saint Hubert, Quebec J3Y 8Y9

Glossary

asteroid: very small "planets" made of rock or metal. There are thousands of asteroids in our Solar System. They mainly orbit the Sun in large numbers between Mars and Jupiter. Some, however, are found in other parts of the Solar System – as meteoroids and possibly as "captured" moons of planets.

atmosphere: the gases that surround a planet, star, or moon.

axis: the imaginary straight line around which a planet, star, or moon turns, or spins.

billion: the number represented by 1 followed by nine zeroes – 1,000,000,000. In some countries, this number is called "a thousand million." In these countries, one billion would then be represented by 1 followed by twelve zeroes – 1,000,000,000,000: a million million.

black hole: a massive object – usually a collapsed star – so tightly packed that not even light can escape the force of its gravity.

captured asteroids: asteroids that have been trapped by the gravity of planets. They then circle the planet.

comet: an object made of ice, rock, and gas. It has a vapor trail that can be seen when it orbits close to the Sun.

constellation: a grouping of stars that seems to trace a familiar pattern or figure. Constellations are often named after the shapes they resemble.

crater: a hole or pit in the surface of a planet or moon caused by a volcanic explosion or the impact of an object.

Galilean satellites: Jupiter's four largest satellites – Io, Europa, Ganymede, and Callisto – that Galileo studied through his telescope. Each of them is about the size of Earth's Moon, or larger.

Galileo: an Italian astronomer who developed the use of the telescope to study the four largest moons of Jupiter, sunspots, mountains on the Moon, the phases of Venus, and many other objects and events in the Universe.

Great Red Spot: the largest of the huge whirling storms that move along the "belts" and "zones" of Jupiter.

helium: a light, colorless gas.

hydrogen: a colorless, odorless gas that is the simplest and lightest of the elements.

satellite: a smaller body that orbits a larger body. Ganymede is Jupiter's largest natural satellite. *Sputnik 1* was Earth's first artificial satellite.

"shepherd" satellite: a small moon that orbits within or near Jupiter's rings. Its weak gravity helps keep ring matter from drifting away from the planet.

sulfur: a pale yellow, nonmetallic element that is used in the medical, chemical and paper industries.

vapor: a gas formed from a solid or liquid. On Earth, clouds are made of water vapor.

zodiac: the band of twelve constellations across the sky that represents the paths of the Sun, the Moon, and all the main planets except Pluto.

Index

Born in 1920, Isaac Asimov came to the United States as a young boy from his native Russia. As a young man, he was a student of biochemistry. In time, he became one of the most productive writers the world has ever known. His books cover a spectrum of topics, including science, history, language theory, fantasy, and science fiction. His brilliant imagination gained him the respect and admiration of adults and children alike. Sadly, Isaac Asimov died shortly after the publication of the first edition of *Isaac Asimov's Library of the Universe.*

The publishers wish to thank the following for permission to reproduce copyright material: front cover, © Julian Baum 1988; 4 (both), AIP Niels Bohr Library; 4-5, Courtesy of Celestron International; 5, AIP Niels Bohr Library; 6-7 (upper), © Garret Moore 1988; 6-7 (lower), 7, © Richard Baum 1988; 8, 9, © Lynette Cook 1988; 10, NASA; 10-11, © John Foster 1988; 12, © Michael Carroll; 12-13, NASA; 13, Jet Propulsion Laboratory; 14, Sabine Huschke/© Gareth Stevens, Inc.; 15 (large), NASA; 15 (inset), © George Peirson 1988; 16-17, 17 (left), Jet Propulsion Laboratory; 17 (right), Matthew Groshek/© Gareth Stevens, Inc.; 18, Jet Propulsion Laboratory; 18-19 (upper), © Ron Miller; 18-19 (lower), NASA; 20, © Michael Carroll; 20-21, © M. P. Kahl/Tom Stack and Associates; 21, NASA; 22, Matthew Groshek/© Gareth Stevens, Inc.; 23 (large), © John Foster 1988; 23 (inset), NASA; 24-25, © Michael Carroll; 26, Jet Propulsion Laboratory/NASA; 27 (upper), © Michael Carroll; 27 (lower left), Space Telescope Science Institute; 27 (lower right), European Southern Observatory (ESO); 28 (inset), © Sally Bensusen 1988; 28-29, © Sally Bensusen 1987.